Recipes from the East

BY

IRMA WALKER ROSS

Illustrations by Baye Mizumura

CHARLES E. TUTTLE COMPANY

RUTLAND : VERMONT : : TOKYO : JAPAN

Representatives

Continental Europe: BOXERBOOKS, INC., Zurich
British Isles: PRENTICE-HALL INTERNATIONAL, INC., London
Australasia: PAUL FLESCH & CO., PTY. LTD., Melbourne
Canada: M. G. HURTIG LTD., Edmonton

Published by the Charles E. Tuttle Company, Inc.
of Rutland, Vermont & Tokyo, Japan with editorial
offices at Suido 1-chome, 2-6, Bunkyo-ku, Tokyo

Library of Congress
Catalog Card No. 58-12109

International Standard Book No. 0-8048-0498-2

First edition, 1955
Nineteenth Printing, 1971

Printed in Japan

To Rex

WHO SUGGESTED THE IDEA
IN THE FIRST PLACE

Author's Foreword

I can't remember when I couldn't cook, nor when the Orient failed to fascinate me. I spent more time in San Francisco's Chinatown as a kid—wandering up the winding alleys looking bug-eyed at the ducks hanging by their necks in the windows of restaurants and watching the eels slithering around in a bucket—than I ever did at home.

The idea of *Recipes from the East* all started when I bundled together some recipes and sent them off as Christmas cards. My friends were so delighted when they saw them that I received several requests for additional copies.

One evening a friend came over to my home for dinner. We had Indian curry that night, and he was fascinated by the condiments we put on top of the curry. The subject came up about cooking, and I showed him my Christmas card. He thought it was clever, showed it to several of his friends, and that was how *Recipes from the East* was born.

Everywhere I go I collect recipes. Many of my friends throughout the Orient have sent me recipes. Changing an Oriental recipe so that a Westerner will enjoy it isn't as easy as it sounds. We experimented and tested the recipes in my home, and had a gay old time doing it.

There are a number of acknowledgements I should like to make, expressing my thanks for favors and help received :

To Mr. Hollington K. Tong, Ambassador to Japan from the Republic of China, for the delicious Chinese recipes.

To my very dear friend Mrs. Masa Kikuchi Kanroji for her help and interest in the translation of the Japanese recipes.

To my friend Mrs. Soon Hae Kim McKinley for the Korean recipes.

To my secretary Miss Etsuko Ueno, who gave of her time in typing and retyping.

To my friends who unknowingly acted as guinea pigs and were kind enough to say they liked my cooking.

And lastly to my daughter, Nancy Elizabeth Ross, who edited the copy.

Recipes

from India 57

from Russia 65

and from All Over 75

Notes for the cook

Japanese eggplant is small in size. Regular eggplant can be substituted; however, the amount required should be cut in half.

Cooking sherry can be substituted for saké.

Aji-no-moto may be used if desired. It is a tasteless white powder that brings out the hidden flavor of the ingredients. Its chemical name is sodium monoglutamate, and it is sold under various trade names in the United States.

1 tbsp. raw ginger is equivalent to ⅛ tsp. of powdered ginger.

Curry paste is preferable to curry powder. The usual rule is 1½ tbsp. of curry paste or powder to 1 lb. of meat. However, the best rule to follow is to use half the amount of paste or powder required, and season to taste.

Grocery stores specializing in imported foods usually carry curry paste.

from Hawaii

Hawaiian Pork

1 lb. pork, cut into cubes
3 green peppers
1 egg
2 tbsp. flour
½ tsp. salt
½ tsp. pepper
1 can chicken bouillon
½ cup pineapple juice
2½ tbsp. cornstarch
2½ tbsp. soy sauce
½ cup sugar
½ cup vinegar

Cut the green pepper into 1″ squares, removing all the seeds, and boil for 10 minutes. Make a batter of egg, flour, salt, and pepper. Dip the pork in the egg batter. Fry slowly in a skillet until a light brown. Drain off the excess fat and add ¼ can of chicken bouillon, green pepper, and pineapple. Simmer for 10 minutes. Make a sauce of the cornstarch, soy sauce, sugar, vinegar, and the remaining chicken bouillon. Cook until clear. Pour over the pork and simmer for 5 minutes. Serve over hot rice. Serves 6.

Chicken Breasts Hawaiian

2 chicken breasts
1 egg, slightly beaten
1 cup finely grated
   bread crumbs
1 tsp. salt
1 cup pineapple juice
2 tbsp. lemon juice
1 tbsp. cornstarch
¼ tsp. curry paste
1 tbsp. sugar
slivered almonds

Split breasts in half. Remove bones, keeping meat in one piece. Dip in egg. Roll in bread crumbs. Season with salt. Pan fry in ¼ inch hot fat in a heavy skillet until brown. Remove fat from pan. Combine juices, cornstarch, curry, and sugar. Pour over chicken. Cover skillet and cook slowly for 20 to 25 minutes. Top with slivered almonds. Serves 4.

Steak Polynesian

12 steaks, ½″ thick
1 cup vinegar
1 cup soy sauce
½ cup saké
1 crushed clove garlic

1 large onion, sliced
¼ cup finely chopped ginger
salt and pepper

Soak the steaks, turning occasionally, in the soy sauce, vinegar, saké, ginger, onions, and garlic for about two hours. Remove the steaks, season with salt and pepper, and charcoal broil. Baste the steaks while broiling with the mixture of soy sauce, vinegar, and saké. Serves 12.

Skewered Prawns Kauai

½ lb. prawns (cooked)
1 cup pineapple juice
½ cup soy sauce
3 tbsp. honey

1 tbsp. butter
1 tbsp. minced ginger
　　root (optional)
1 ½ tbsp. cornstarch
pepper

Place the pineapple juice, soy sauce, honey, butter, pepper, and ginger in a pan and bring to a boil. Thicken with cornstarch. Place the prawns on skewers, dip in sauce, and broil for a few minutes on each side. Serves 4.

Baked Hawaiian Hash

2 tbsp. brown sugar
2 tbsp. butter
½ tsp. prepared mustard
1 tsp. finely chopped ginger root

2 cups chopped cooked ham
2 cups cubed cooked sweet potatoes
½ cup pineapple juice
4 slices pineapple

Combine ham, sweet potatoes, mustard, ginger, and pineapple juice. Pour into a buttered casserole. Lay half-slices of pineapple on top. Sprinkle with sugar. Dot with butter. Bake in a moderate oven about 30 minutes. Serves 4.

Hawaii ~ 7

Hawaiian Hamburger

1 lb. round steak, ground
1 large onion, finely
   chopped
1 clove garlic, chopped fine
½ cup soy sauce
½ tsp. finely chopped
   ginger root

Mix beef and onions and form into 8 patties. Combine soy sauce, garlic, and ginger, and pour over patties, allowing the meat to stand in this mixture for about half an hour. Remove from the sauce and broil about 7 minutes on each side. Serves 4.

Pork Chops Hawaiian

6 thick pork chops
1 cup pineapple, diced
1 cup pineapple juice
1 bay leaf
1 cup chopped celery

1 tsp. ground cloves
1 clove of garlic, cut fine
½ tsp. Aji-no-moto
salt and pepper

Salt and pepper the pork chops and brown in skillet. After the chops have been browned, spread the diced pineapple over each chop. Add pineapple juice and the other ingredients. Simmer until done. Serves 6.

from Japan

Steam in a Tea Cup
(Chawan-Mushi)

1/3 lb. sliced chicken

12 shrimps, cut in small pieces

3 tbsp. soy sauce

30 chestnuts or walnuts

6 dried mushrooms

½ tsp. saké or cooking sherry

4 eggs

3 cups chicken soup stock

½ tsp. salt

3 stalks finely chopped spinach

1 finely chopped lemon rind

Soak the chicken and shrimps in 1 tbsp. soy sauce for a short time. Cut up nuts and boil mushrooms, nuts, 4 tbsp. chicken soup stock, ½ tsp. soy sauce, and saké with chicken and shrimps for about ten minutes. Beat the eggs; add balance of soup stock, 2 tbsp. soy sauce, and salt. Divide the boiled ingredients into 6 small bowls and pour the egg mixture over it. Sprinkle the spinach and lemon rind sparingly over the top. Place the bowls in a steam kettle, cover the top, and boil for about 15 minutes. Serves 6.

Japan ~ 13

Barbarian Duck
(Kamo-Nanban)

1 lb. cooked duck or chicken meat, sliced thin
3 long green onions, cut in 1" lengths
½ can bamboo shoots, sliced thin
3 cups chicken stock or 1 ½ cans chicken soup
½ cup soy sauce
5 tbsp. saké or cooking sherry
2 tbsp. sugar
1 pinch Aji-no-moto

Bring to a boil the chicken stock, soy sauce, saké, sugar, and Aji-no-moto. Add the bamboo shoots and duck to the liquid and cook until done. Add the green onions. Boil for 5 minutes. Serve very hot over cooked noodles. Serves 6.

Mother and Son
(Oyako-Domburi)

1/3 lb. sliced cooked
  chicken
1/2 lb. mushrooms
3 onions
1 cup chicken stock
6 tbsp. soy sauce
6 tbsp. sherry or saké
6 eggs
1 1/2 lbs. boiled rice

Slice the chicken thin. Slice the mushrooms into pieces 1 1/2" long; slice the onions lengthwise. Boil the sherry, soup stock, and soy sauce. Put the chicken, mushrooms, and onions into it. Divide this into 6 portions after it is boiled. Put 1 portion into a frying pan and set on the stove. Beat an egg lightly and add it to the pan. When the egg is half cooked, transfer all the ingredients into an individual bowl of hot rice. Repeat this 6 times, as each portion is cooked separately. Serves 6.

Bird of Fire
(Yakitori)

1 ½ lbs. chicken meat, cut
   in large cubes
1 cup saké or cooking
   sherry
1 cup soy sauce
3 tbsp. sugar
2 tsp. pepper

To make sauce, mix saké, soy sauce, sugar, and pepper
and simmer for about 15 minutes. Place chicken on
skewers and broil meat slightly. Brush on sauce and
broil again. Repeat this several times. Sprinkle pepper
on the meat before serving. Serves 6.

Shrimp Tempura

1 lb. large shrimps or
    prawns
1 egg
½ cup water
¼ cup flour
¾ cup soup stock or
    canned consommé
5 tbsp. soy sauce
3 tsp. sherry or sweet saké
grated horseradish or
    ginger

Mix the egg and water in a bowl. Add the unsifted
flour; stir thoroughly, but do not try to get out the
lumps. Use the batter immediately after mixing; do not
let it stand. Dip shrimps in batter and fry in deep fat.
To prepare sauce, bring to a boil the soup stock, soy
sauce, and saké. Do not let shrimps stand after frying.
Serve with sauce and grated horseradish or ginger.
Serves 6.

Fish with Chrysanthemum Cucumber

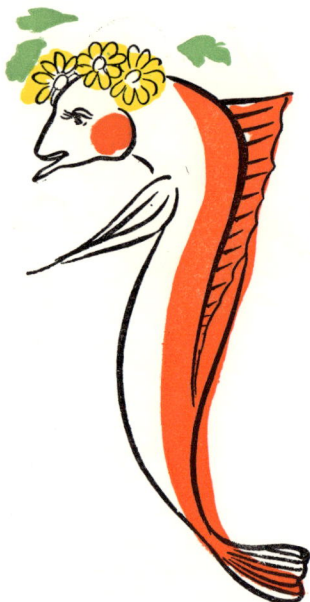

6 small slices of fish
7 tsp. salt
4 tbsp. soy sauce
5 tbsp. sherry or sweet saké
1 tbsp. vinegar
½ tbsp. sugar
6 small cucumbers
1 red pepper

Soak the fish in ½ cup of soy sauce 2 hours prior to broiling. Remove from soy sauce and sprinkle salt on both sides of fish; then broil on skewers until both sides of fish are a golden brown. Remove from broiler and dip in a mixture of 4 tbsp. of soy sauce and 4 tbsp. of sherry or sweet saké. Repeat this three times; then remove from broiler. Be careful not to burn the fish. Remove the skin from the cucumbers; then slice lengthwise in ½″ slices, then sideways, but not through. Sprinkle salt sparingly on the cucumber to soften it. Soak for about an hour in a sauce of 1 tbsp. vinegar, 1 tbsp. sherry, and ½ tbsp. sugar. Arrange the cucumber to resemble a chrysanthemum. Place in the center of the cucumber a small amount of finely chopped red pepper and serve as garnish with fish.

Sukiyaki

1½ lbs. steak, cut in thin strips

2 tbsp. salad oil

¼ cup sugar

¾ cup soy sauce

¼ cup water, or mushroom stock

2 medium onions, sliced

1 green pepper, sliced in thin strips

1 cup 1½" strips of celery

1 can bamboo shoots, sliced thin

1 can mushrooms, sliced thin

1 bunch green onions, cut in 1" lengths, including the tops

Heat oil in skillet, add meat, and brown lightly. Mix sugar, soy sauce, and mushroom stock. Cook half of this with the meat. Push meat to one side of pan and add sliced onions, green pepper, and celery. Cook a few minutes; add remaining soy sauce mixture, bamboo shoots, and mushrooms. Cook 3 to 5 minutes. Add green onions. Cook 1 minute more, then add ½ cup of saké if desired. Cook 1 minute, stir well, and serve immediately over hot rice. Serves 8.

Japan ~ 19

Salt Grilled Fish with Ginger

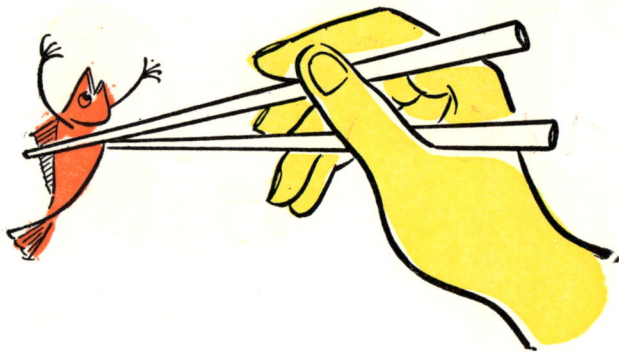

6 small white fish
2 tbsp. finely cut ginger
root

2 tbsp. vinegar
1 tsp. salt
6 tbsp. soy sauce

Scale the fish, remove gills, and salt both sides. Place fish on skewers and grill. Grill thoroughly on both sides until well done. Serve with sauce made of ginger root, vinegar, salt, and soy sauce. Serves 6.

Nihon Chicken with Bamboo

1 lb. chopped cooked chicken
5 tbsp. sherry
1 tbsp. soy sauce
6 prawns
½ cup peas
1 ½ lbs. bamboo shoots
6 dried or fresh mushrooms
1 cup soup stock or canned chicken soup
4 tbsp. sugar
½ tsp. salt

Boil prawns in salted water and remove shells. Boil prawns, soup stock, sugar, and salt for 5 minutes. After boiling fresh peas in salted water, add them to the prawns and soup stock. Cut chicken in small pieces and boil in this mixture, adding 5 tbsp. of sherry and 1 tbsp. of soy sauce. Cut the bamboo shoots into lengthwise pieces; add them and whole mushrooms to the mixture; heat thoroughly. Serve over hot rice. Serves 6.

Broiled Lamb Chops a la Nihon

4 1½″ lamb chops
½ cup soy sauce
½ cup water

1 clove garlic, cut fine
1 tbsp. chopped ginger
  root

Put chops in a casserole. Make a sauce of garlic, soy sauce, and water, pour over chops, and let stand overnight in the refrigerator. Place chops in broiler and pour remaining sauce and ginger over them. Broil for 10 minutes. Brown on both sides. Serve with hot rice. Serves 4.

Nihon Chicken with Snow Peas

½ lb. chicken
6 dried mushrooms (or
  canned)
1 onion
1 ½ tbsp. oil
½ lb. snow peas (or
  fresh peas)
a little spinach
3 eggs
3 tbsp. sherry
4 tbsp. sugar
1 tsp. salt
3 tbsp. soy sauce
4 tbsp. soup stock

Slice chicken, mushrooms, and onion. Boil snow peas in salted water. Cut the spinach in 1" pieces. Lightly fry mushrooms and onion, adding soup stock, sherry, sugar, salt, and soy sauce. Add chicken meat. Cover the dish with a lid and place in a steam kettle over a medium flame. When liquid decreases, add peas and spinach. Beat eggs and spread over the top. When it hardens, remove from stove. Cut into wedges like a pie. Serves 6.

Nihon Eggplant

6 small Japanese egg-
  plants
1 can tomato sauce
1 large onion, chopped
  fine
salt and pepper to taste

Peel the eggplant and cut into small cubes. Place a
small amount of oil in a saucepan and add the eggplant,
tomato sauce, chopped onions, salt, and pepper. Cook
until the eggplant is soft; if needed, add a small amount
of water. Serves 6.

Teriyaki

2 lbs. salmon, thinly sliced

1 tbsp. finely chopped fresh ginger root

2 cloves garlic, chopped fine

1 medium onion, chopped fine

2 tbsp. sugar

½ cup soy sauce

¼ cup water

Cut salmon into serving pieces. Make a sauce from ginger root, garlic, onion, sugar, soy sauce, and water. Pour over fish. Let stand 1 to 2 hours. Spread fish out on a shallow pan and broil 3 to 5 minutes on each side. Serve hot. Serves 6.

Pink Flower Egg

4 eggs
1 tsp. soy sauce
1 tsp. prepared mustard
a dash of pepper
a little red coloring

Boil eggs; mash the yolk and white separately. Add red coloring to the white of the egg, making it slightly pink in color. Add a dash of pepper, soy sauce, and mustard to the yolk. Place a dry napkin on a flexible table mat, spread the white of the egg over it, and then spread the yolk over the white of the egg. Roll the mat and tie at each end with string. Steam in a kettle for about 15 minutes. Cool the roll and slice. This is nice served on crackers and used as an appetizer.

Chicken Rice

3 cups rice
5½ cups chicken stock
  (or canned chicken
  soup)

½ lb. chicken
5 tbsp. soy sauce
5 tbsp. sherry

Cut the chicken into small pieces and dip in a mixture of soy sauce and sherry. After removing the chicken from the mixture of soy sauce and sherry, add the chicken stock. Place the uncooked rice into the mixture and boil. After the rice has boiled, add the chicken. Cook until done. Let stand for a few minutes, then thoroughly mix before serving. Serves 6.

Nihon Egg Rolls

2 cups cooked rice
1 can tuna fish
2 eggs
salt and pepper to taste

½ tsp. curry powder or
  paste
½ small onion, chopped
  fine

Place the rice in a bowl.
Add flaked tuna, eggs, and
chopped onion.   Stir thoroughly, then add the seasoning.   Form into balls and fry.
Makes 10 balls.

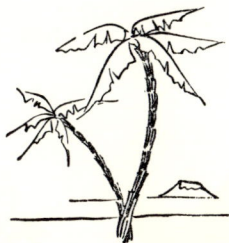

from the Philippines

Beef a la Baguio

2 cups chopped cooked beef (perhaps a left-over roast)
3 chopped onions
1 can tomato sauce
½ can water
1 clove garlic
2 tbsp. chopped parsley
1 pinch thyme
1 pinch saffron
1 bay leaf
½ tsp. Aji-no-moto
1½ tbsp. butter

Brown the onions in butter and add the tomato sauce, water, garlic, thyme, saffron, bay leaf, and Aji-no-moto. To this, add 1½ cups of washed, uncooked rice and simmer until the rice begins to swell. Add the chopped beef and simmer until done. Salt and pepper to taste. Serves 6.

Spiced Pork

5 lb. leg of pork
1 cup vinegar
1 tbsp. salt
1 tsp. black pepper
2 buds garlic
1 large onion

Place pork in a kettle and pour vinegar over pork. Season thoroughly with salt and pepper. Add garlic and chopped onion. Allow pork to stand in this mixture for 1 hour. Turn occasionally so that pork is well soaked. Remove from kettle and place in baking pan. Pour mixture over pork; baste. Bake until done. Serve with applesauce that has been flavored with red cinnamon candy hearts. Serves 10.

Crab Manila

2 cups cooked (or canned) crab meat
2 eggs, well-beaten
¼ tbsp. minced onion
2 cups ground ham
¼ cup chopped walnuts
4 tbsp. soy sauce
4 tbsp. oil
½ cup water
2 tbsp. cornstarch
1 tbsp. finely chopped ginger
pepper

Brown the ham over a low flame. Add the onion and pepper. Blend the cornstarch and water and add to the ham. Gradually stir in the beaten eggs; then add the soy sauce, ginger, and walnuts. Cook slowly for five minutes. Heat the crab meat in another pan and, when hot, add to the sauce. Serve over rice. Serves 6.

Adabo

1 chicken (large)
$1/8$ cup vinegar
2 tsp. salt
$3/4$ tsp. pepper

Cut chicken in pieces and place in a kettle containing enough water to cover the chicken. Add vinegar, salt, and pepper and boil until done. Drain. Dredge the chicken in flour and fry until a golden brown. Make a paste of flour and water and add to soup stock. Simmer until the stock thickens. Serve as gravy over mashed potatoes. Serves 5.

Philippine Fish and String Beans

1 can tuna	salt and pepper
2 tbsp. shrimps	water
1 large tomato	1 lb. fresh string beans

Parboil the string beans. Drain the water from the beans when partially done. Cut tomato in pieces and add to beans. Add fish, seasoning, shrimps, and a small amount of water. Cook until the beans are done. Serves 6.

Adobong Isda

1 ½ lbs. fish (halibut or white fish)
1 tsp. salt
2 buds finely chopped garlic
½ cup chopped onion
2 bay leaves
2 green peppers, cut in large pieces
1 can tomato sauce
5 tbsp. vinegar

Place the fish in a baking pan. Rub on both sides with a small amount of salt. Place 2 tbsp. of salad oil in baking dish. Add garlic, onions, bay leaves, peppers, tomato sauce, and vinegar. Baste occasionally and bake until done. Serves 6.

Fish a la Mindanao

2 lbs. fish (white)
½ cup salad oil
1 clove garlic
1 medium onion, cut in small pieces

2 medium sized tomatoes
salt and pepper to taste
1 tsp. Spanish pepper
1 egg

Cut fish in individual pieces and deep fry until a golden brown. Make sauce as follows: mince garlic, add onions and cubed tomatoes, boil the vegetables in 1 cup of water until soft. Press through a sieve. Add 1 beaten egg to the liquid. Simmer until the liquid thickens. Pour over fried fish. Serves 8.

from China

Fried Diced Chicken with Walnuts

½ chicken
6 mushrooms (big)
1 cup walnuts
2 tbsp. soy sauce
½ tbsp. cornstarch
1 tsp. salt
½ tsp. sugar
1 cup cooking oil

Shell and dice the walnuts. Heat the oil and fry the nuts until they are a golden brown. Remove from the fire and blot on heavy Manila paper. Clean and dice the chicken and place about 4 tbsp. of oil in a frying pan, pouring in the diced chicken when the oil is smoking hot. Stir for one minute. Have the cornstarch, sugar, salt, and soy sauce thoroughly mixed together and pour the mixture over the frying chicken. Soak the mushrooms in hot water for about 10 minutes and dice them. Add them to the mixture in the frying pan and stir for 5 minutes until the mushrooms are tender. Remove from fire. Mix in the deep-fried walnuts before serving. Serves 4.

Fish Balls

1 ½ fish, white
1 slice ginger
2 tsp. cornstarch
1 tsp. pepper
2 small spring onions

Remove head of fish; split down the back into two halves. With a spoon, scrape the inside from the tail toward the head. Chop fish finely with spring onions and ginger. Dissolve ½ tsp. salt in a cup of water and add gradually to the meat. Add pepper and cornstarch and mix thoroughly again. Take a fistful of the seasoned fish and squeeze it out through the hole formed by the index finger and the thumb and scoop with a spoon. Put balls thus formed into hot water and boil for 3 minutes. They can be stored in a refrigerator for days. They may be fried in deep oil until brown and served with a sweet and sour sauce and pickles. The fish balls may be cooked with mushrooms and bamboo shoots. They can also be added to chicken or meat soup or to the stock in which the fish balls were cooked. By adding 1 ½ tsp. salt and 1 tbsp. of lard to a few cabbage hearts, mushrooms, and bamboo shoots, a delicious soup is made. Serves 6.

Roast Duck

1 duck
1 cup sherry
2 tbsp. salt

Pluck and wash the duck till it is thoroughly clean. Remove the oil sacs. Place it in a heavy pot with salt and wine. Cook on a low fire for ½ hour. Remove from the pot and place in a pan and bake in a moderate oven for about 20 minutes or until the duck is brown. Stick a fork through the duck. It will easily go through if it is done. Serve with sweet soy jam if available. Serves 6.

Shark's Fin Soup

½ lb. skinless fins
3 rice bowls chicken soup

½ tbsp. salt
2 oz. ham, cooked

Warm the chicken (or meat) soup. Add ½ tbsp. salt. Soak shark's fins in warm water for about 10 minutes to soften; add to soup and cook for 10 minutes. Sprinkle minced ham on top of soup before serving. Serves 4.

Egg Dumplings

6 eggs
½ lb. of pork
3 tsp. soy sauce
1 tsp. sugar
1 tsp. salt
2 or 3 spring onions
2 or 3 slices of ginger
cooking oil

Throughly mince the meat, spring onions, and ginger and mix them with 1½ tsp. soy sauce. Beat the eggs and add the salt. Drop 2 tsp. of cooking oil in the frying pan and when hot, drop 1 tbsp. of the beaten egg in the center of the pan in the same manner as with griddle cakes. Immediately place 1 tsp. of meat mixture in the center of the egg, fold over, press down edges, and remove from pan. Repeat the same process until all the ingredients are used up. When all have been cooked, replace in pan. Add ½ cup of water and remaining 1½ tsp. soy sauce and sugar. Cover tightly and cook slowly for 10 minutes and serve. Serves 6.

Meat Balls with a College Education

1 lb. round steak, ground
1 egg
2 tbsp. flour
1 tsp. salt
1 ½ tbsp. onion, chopped fine
3 green peppers, cut in large pieces
salt and pepper to taste
4 slices of pineapple, cut into cubes
1 cup chicken stock or canned chicken coup
3 tbsp. cornstarch
2 tsp. soy sauce
½ cup vinegar
½ cup sugar

Mix the meat, egg, salt and pepper, and onions. Make into balls, roll in flour, and fry until a light brown. After meat is browned, add ⅓ cup chicken stock, 1 tbsp. oil, cubed pineapple, and green peppers. Simmer over low flame for a few minutes. Make a sauce of cornstarch, soy sauce, vinegar, sugar, and ⅔ cup chicken stock. Stir well. Add to the meat balls. Heat thoroughly. Serves 6.

Sweet Sour Fish

Clean fish; make diagonal slashes on each side, leaving the flesh adhering to the bones. Dredge well with the cornstarch paste. Heat pan, add oil, hold the fish over the pan of deep fat, and baste the slashes with the hot oil until brown. Then fry in deep fat until crisp. Prepare sweet and sour sauce by mixing oil, sugar, cornstarch, soy sauce, and vinegar. Add onions and ginger and boil for a few minutes. Pour over fish. Serves 6.

1 3 lb. fish, white
3 cups of oil
cornstarch paste
3 tbsp. oil
1 cup sugar
2 tbsp. cornstarch
4 tbsp. soy sauce
2 cups mild vinegar
1 large onion, chopped fine
3 tbsp. chopped ginger

Pregnant Cucumber

1 lb. pork, ground
1 tbsp. oil
1 tsp. salt
1 tbsp. soy sauce
1 tbsp. cornstarch
1 tbsp. onions, finely diced
1 cup celery, finely diced
1 tbsp. chopped ginger
4 large cucumbers
1 can beef bouillon or bouillon cube
sauce consisting of:
  2 tbsp. cornstarch
  2 tbsp. soy sauce
  ½ cup water

Remove half the peeling from the cucumbers; cut in 2" slices; scoop out seeds. Mix the pork, salt, soy sauce, cornstarch, onions, celery, ginger, and oil. Fill the cucumber slices. Place 2 tbsp. of oil in a large pan; place the stuffed cucumbers and bouillon in pan. Cover the pan and cook for about 10 minutes. Simmer for about 35 minutes. Pour sauce over cucumbers and serve at once. Serves 6.

Formosan Pork

½ lb. pork, cut in small pieces

3 onions, chopped fine

½ head cabbage, finely shredded

3 green peppers, cut in small pieces

3 tbsp. soy sauce

1 tbsp. ginger, chopped fine

1 tsp. sugar

a pinch of salt

3 tbsp. oil

Heat oil in pan; add meat and onions. Fry until well done. Add soy sauce and cabbage; cook until cabbage is done. Add ginger, peppers, salt, and sugar. Serve over hot rice. Serves 6.

Peppered Chicken

1 lb. chicken, cut into 2" pieces
1 cup oil
1 cup chopped onion
1 cucumber
1 red pepper (hot)
1 green pepper
2 red sweet peppers
3 tbsp. cornstarch
4 tbsp. soy sauce
1 tsp. sugar
½ tsp. salt
¼ cup soup stock

Dredge the chicken in a mixture of 1 tbsp. cornstarch and 1 tbsp. soy sauce; fry until a golden brown. Dredge cubed onion, cucumber, and peppers in a mixture of 2 tbsp. cornstarch, 3 tbsp. soy sauce, sugar, salt, and soup stock. Fry in 2 tbsp. of oil. Combine the meat and vegetables. Serves 6.

Shrimp Foo Yung

1 cup shrimps, fresh or canned

1 cup onions, chopped fine

¼ cup water chestnuts, sliced thin

½ cup mushrooms, sliced thin

5 eggs

3 tbsp. soy sauce

1 tbsp. cornstarch

¼ cup bouillon

¼ tsp. sugar

To make the foo yung, beat eggs with shrimps, onions, chestnuts, and mushrooms until thick. Add 2 tbsp. soy sauce and continue to beat. Place a small amount of oil in a shallow pan; when the pan is hot enough, pour the mixture into the pan. Brown on both sides. Serve hot with sauce made by simmering the following ingredients over a low flame: 1 tbsp. soy sauce, cornstarch, bouillon, and sugar. Serves 6.

Beef and Onions

3 large onions, chopped fine
½ lb. beef, cut in thin strips
4 tbsp. oil
2 tbsp. soy sauce
½ tsp. sugar
½ tsp. salt
2 tsp. sherry
2 tsp. cornstarch

Dredge the meat in cornstarch, 1 tbsp. soy sauce, ¼ tsp. salt, and 1 tsp. sherry. Sauté the meat in 2 tbsp. of oil. Fry the onions, ¼ tsp. salt, 1 tbsp. soy sauce, sugar, and 1 tsp. sherry for a few seconds. Add the sautéed beef and thoroughly heat. Serves 6.

Spareribs with Sweet Sour Sauce

1 lb. spareribs of pork, cut
  into 2″ pieces
2 tsp. soy sauce
3 tbsp. cornstarch
2 cups oil
½ cup cold water
1 medium-sized onion,
  sliced fine
¾ cup sugar
1 cup mild vinegar
¼ cup soy sauce

Place the spareribs in a kettle containing ½ cup of cold
water. Boil for 20 minutes. Dredge the spareribs in a
mixture of 1 tbsp. cornstarch and 2 tsp. soy sauce. Fry
the spareribs until brown in a very hot skillet. Sauté
the onions. Prepare sweet and sour sauce by mixing
sugar, vinegar, ¼ cup soy sauce, and 2 tbsp. cornstarch.
Add spareribs and onions to sauce and heat thoroughly.
Serves 6.

Spring Rolls

8 large mushrooms, fresh
  or dried
1 onion, chopped fine
½ can bamboo shoots
½ lb. bean sprouts
1 tbsp. ginger, chopped
  fine
½ lb. lean ground pork,
  dredged with :
  1 tbsp. soy sauce
  1 tbsp. sherry
  1 tsp. salt
  1 tbsp. cornstarch

Cut bamboo shoots and mushrooms; sauté them; then add 3 tbsp. soy sauce. Sauté onions and mushrooms. Sauté the pork with the vegetables and ginger. Spread 1½ tbsp. of the pork and vegetable mixture on a pancake. Fold sides and roll, moistening the edges with water to hold them together. Fry the rolls in deep fat until brown. To prepare pancake batter, beat 6 eggs, 2 cups water, 2 cups flour, and 1 tsp. salt. Heat a small frying pan with ½ tsp. of oil; pour a very small amount of batter in the bottom of pan. The pancake should be very thin; it should cook less than a minute, only long enough to set. Continue until the desired number is reached. Serves 6.

Ch'ao Mien

Brown pork, season, then add fat, sliced onion, celery, mushrooms, drained bean sprouts, and bamboo shoots. Cook until vegetables are golden brown. Add water and simmer 20 to 30 minutes. Slowly stir in flour blended with water. Cook 10 minutes. Add sugar and soy sauce to taste. Top with toasted almonds. Serve hot over fried noodles. Serves 6.

1 lb. pork, diced
1 tsp. salt
2 tbsp. fat
1 medium onion
1 cup finely chopped celery
½ cup mushrooms, thinly sliced
1 can bean sprouts
1 can bamboo shoots
2 cups water
1 tbsp. flour
1 tbsp. water
1 tbsp. sugar
2 tbsp. soy sauce
¼ cup toasted almonds

from India

Indian Curry

Melt butter in a frying pan, add sliced onions and chili peppers, and fry until a brownish color. Add curry paste. Add meat, after cutting into small pieces. Stir constantly for 15 minutes, making sure the contents do not burn. When th's mixture has been well cooked, add 1 pint of water and salt to taste. Cover pan and boil for 15 minutes. The liquid will slowly thicken. Serve over hot rice. Serves 6.

1 lb. meat (beef)
8 oz. sliced onions
3 oz. butter
2 red chili peppers
pinch of salt
1½ tbsp. curry paste
1 pint water

Chicken Curry

3 chickens
1 cup curry paste
1 can tomato sauce
7 large onions
1 ½ cloves garlic
2 red chili peppers
6 tsp. salt
1 tbsp. sugar
¼ tsp. white pepper

To make soup stock, boil wings, back, neck, and gizzard of the chickens. Fry chopped onions, peppers, and garlic until well browned. Cut the chicken into pieces and fry. After the chicken has been fried, place in a large kettle, adding the onions, peppers, and garlic. Place 1 tbsp. of salad oil in a skillet, add the curry paste and tomato sauce, and fry, stirring constantly, for 15 minutes; then add 3 cups of chicken soup stock. Cook for 5 minutes; then add to the fried chicken. Add the rest of the soup stock to the chicken and cook in an open kettle for 1 ½ hours, or until the chicken is done. Serve over hot rice. Sprinkle the following condiments on top of the curry, layer on layer: salted peanuts, India relish, pickled onions, ginger, chutney, grated coconut, chopped ham, grated eggs. Serves 6.

Curried Salmon

1 large onion, chopped
fine

1 can tomato sauce

1 can salmon (remove
small bones)

2 tbsp. curry paste

salt and pepper to taste

½ cup water

1 ½ tbsp. oil

Fry the onion in oil until a
light brown. Add the tomato
sauce, water, salmon, curry
paste, and salt and pepper.
Simmer until mixture thickens.
Serve over hot rice. Serves
6.

Curried Veal

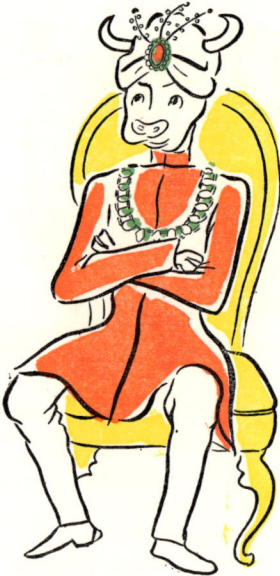

2 lbs. lean veal, cubed
2 onions, sliced thin
3 tbsp. butter
1 tbsp. curry paste
1½ cups boiling water
1 tsp. lemon juice

Add the cubed veal and onions to the melted fat and cook in a skillet for 3 minutes, but do not brown. Add curry paste and salt and cook for another 2 minutes. Add water and simmer until meat is done. To thicken, add a little flour, if desired. Add the lemon juice just before serving. Serve over hot rice. Serves 6.

Indian Beef Stew

Dredge the cubed beef in a combination of flour, salt, and pepper. Fry the beef in a skillet until a light brown. Add water ; simmer about 1 hour. Add onions and green pepper and continue to cook for about 30 minutes. Combine sour cream, curry paste, and cayenne pepper, stir into the stew, and cook for 1 minute. Season to taste. Serve over hot rice. Serves 4.

1 lb. lean stew meat or chuck roast, cut into 1½" cubes.
¼ cup flour
1 tsp. salt
⅛ tsp. black pepper
¼ cup fat
4 small onions, peeled
1 green pepper, sliced
1 cup sour cream
2 tsp. curry paste
⅛ tsp. cayenne pepper

India ~ 63

Curried Chicken Patties

2 lbs. uncooked chicken,
    chopped
1 large onion, chopped
    fine
1 hard-boiled egg
1 tsp. curry paste
salt to taste

Grind (using the coarse grind) onion, egg, and chicken;
add curry paste and salt. Place in the refrigerator
overnight. Form into small patties and fry in deep fat.
Serves 6.

from Russia

Beef Stroganoff

1 ½ lbs. steak, cut in ½" strips
¼ cup flour
1 tsp. salt
2 small onions, chopped fine
½ lb. mushrooms, cut in small pieces
1 clove garlic, chopped fine
3 tbsp. fat
2 tbsp. flour
1 can beef bouillon
1 tbsp. Worcestershire sauce
1 cup sour cream

Dredge steak in flour and salt. Fry onions, mushrooms, and garlic in fat for 5 minutes. Add steak, brown; then remove meat, onions, and mushrooms from pan. Mix 2 tbsp. flour with the drippings; add bouillon and Worcestershire sauce. Cook until thickened. Add sour cream and heat until gravy begins to simmer. Add the meat and vegetables; continue to cook until piping hot. Serve over hot cooked rice. Serves 6.

Russia ~ 67

Lamb a la Russian

1 lb. cubed lamb
4 slices bacon
salt and pepper
8 small onions

Cut lamb and bacon into 1" pieces. Alternate lamb, bacon, and onions on 4 skewers. Broil about 15 minutes, turning to brown evenly. Season with salt and pepper. Serve with Sweet and Sour Cabbage, which is made by mixing and cooking until soft the following ingredients: 1 small head red cabbage, shredded; 2 apples, diced; ½ cup vinegar; ¼ cup sugar; salt and pepper to taste.

Ham Pilof

1 ½ cups slivered ham
¾ cup uncooked rice
2 tbsp. butter
2 cups hot bouillon
1 tbsp. chopped onion
2 tsp. Worcestershire sauce

Wash rice thoroughly. Melt butter in heavy skillet. Add rice and heat until golden brown. Add bouillon, onion, and Worcestershire sauce. Heat to boiling. Add meat and place in casserole. Bake in a moderate oven about 40 minutes. Serves 4.

Borscht

1 ¼ lbs. beef bones
3 quarts water
1 lb. bacon
3 carrots
12 medium-sized beets
3 stalks celery
1 cup shredded cabbage
2 onions
6 sprigs parsley
2 cloves garlic
1 tsp. thyme
1 bay leaf
salt and pepper

Make soup stock by boiling beef bones in water with a dash of salt. Into the soup stock, place a small bag containing chopped garlic, parsley, bay leaf, and thyme. Chop fine all vegetables and bacon and place in soup stock. When the vegetables have been thoroughly cooked, strain the stock. Beat stiffly 3 egg whites, fold gently into the stock, and cook for an additional 15 minutes. To serve, add 1 tbsp. whipped cream to each portion with a dash of horseradish. Serves 8.

Russian Cabbage Rolls

1 lb. round steak, ground
½ lb. ground pork
3 cups cooked rice
1 tsp. sugar
1 onion, chopped
1 tsp. salt
¼ tsp. pepper
1 head cabbage
1 tbsp. butter
1 cup hot water
1 can cream of tomato soup

Combine the beef, pork, rice, sugar, onion, salt, and pepper. Place cabbage leaves in boiling hot water for a few minutes. Roll inside individual cabbage leaves the mixture of beef, pork, rice, sugar, onion, salt, and pepper. Place rolled cabbage leaves in baking pan. Dot each with butter. Combine soup and water and pour over the rolls. Bake in moderate oven 1 hour. Serves 6.

Russian Grill

1 ½ lbs. cubed lamb
½ cup French dressing
1 clove garlic
½ lb. button mushrooms (canned)
4 slices bacon
1 tsp. salt
¼ tsp pepper

Add chopped garlic to the French dressing; pour dressing over the cubed lamb; let stand 1 hour in the refrigerator. Cut bacon into 1" pieces. Alternate lamb, bacon, and mushrooms on metal skewers. Allow space between for through cooking. Season with salt and pepper. Broil about 15 minutes. Serves 6.

Russian Eggplant Caviar

1 eggplant
2 onions, chopped fine
5 tomatoes

parsley
salt and pepper to taste

Place the eggplant in a pan
and bake until soft. Remove
skin from eggplant and chop
fine. Fry the onions until a
golden brown; add tomatoes,
eggplant, parsley, and
seasoning. Cook until thick.
Serve cold on lettuce.

Piroshki

2 chopped onions
½ lb. ground beef
½ cup chopped mushrooms
salt and pepper to taste

Fry onions until a light brown; add meat; brown slightly. Add chopped mushrooms and seasoning. Make a rich flaky pie dough, by mixing ½ cup butter, ½ cup of sour cream, 1 egg, and 1¼ cups flour or enough to absorb the moisture. Cut in 3″ squares. Spoon mixture into the squares. Fold over and seal with water. Bake in oven for 25 minutes. Serve with rich gravy made from canned mushroom soup.

74 ~ Russia

and from

All Over

Spring Kim Chee

3 heads cabbage
3 tbsp. salt
3 green onions
1 clove garlic
1 tbsp. chopped chili pepper
1 tbsp. chopped candied ginger
1 ½ cups water

Wash cabbage and cut into strips 1″ wide and 2″ long. Sprinkle with 2 tbsp. salt and let stand for half an hour. Cut onions, including tops, into 1½″ lengths and shred. Chop garlic, red pepper, and ginger into fine pieces. After cabbage has set for 30 minutes, wash twice in cold water. Mix prepared vegetables with cabbage, add 1 tbsp. of salt and enough water to cover the cabbage, and let stand for 7 days in covered crock.

Korea ~ ㄱㄱ

Korean Chop Chai

¾ lbs. beef, cut into ¼"
   slices
1 large carrot
1 lb. dried mushrooms (flat
   type)
1 lb. Chinese noodles
½ bunch spinach
1 large onion
½ cup soy sauce
1 tbsp. sesame seed
1 tbsp. sugar
5 tbsp. salad oil

Slice all vegetables into ¼" slices. Fry each vegetable
separately, adding a small portion of beef. Prior to
frying, soak dried mushrooms in a small amount of cold
water. When mushrooms are softened, fry as before.
Soak noodles in hot water for about 5 minutes. Mix
all vegetables, meat, and noodles in a kettle; season
with sesame seed and soy sauce. Cook for 5 minutes.
Serve either hot or cold as desired. Serves 6.

Spinach Namnol

1 ½ lbs. spinach
¼ lb. beef
dash red pepper
1 green onion
1 clove garlic
1 tbsp. roasted sesame
  seed
2 tbsp. soy sauce
1 tbsp. sugar
1 tbsp. salad oil

Wash spinach well and cook in a little water until tender. Drain well and cut into 2″ pieces. Chop beef fine and add pepper. Chop onion, including tops, and mix with sesame seed, soy sauce, sugar, and oil. Cook meat until seared. Mix meat with spinach and other ingredients and season with salt. Serve hot.

Korean Kolbe (Braised Beef)

3 lbs. beef (chuck roast), cut into six pieces
1 clove garlic
5 green onions
2 tbsp. sesame seed
1 cup soy sauce
1 tbsp. sugar
1 tsp. Aji-no-moto
1 egg

Place beef in kettle; cover with water; place over a medium flame and cook until meat is soft enough to stick with a fork (approximately 3 hours). After meat has been cooking for about 2 hours, add minced garlic, sugar, and soy sauce; cook until soy sauce permeates the meat (approximately 1 hour). Cut green onions into 1" lengths; place over meat. Sprinkle sesame seed and Aji-no-moto; steam over a low flame until all that remains of the water in the kettle is a thick gravy. Separate the yolk from the white of the egg. Whip the white of egg until it is stiff; add the yolk. Heat a frying pan; add a small amount of oil; fry the egg mixture. Upon completion of the frying, cut the egg into fine strips. When serving the beef and gravy, place fine strips of egg over the top. Serves 6.

Siamese Fried Rice

2 cups cooked rice
1 large onion
2 eggs
1 green pepper
½ cup chopped cooked
  ham (or shrimps)
salt and pepper

Chop onion in small pieces and fry until a golden brown. Remove from pan, chop green pepper into small pieces, and fry until done. Remove the green pepper from pan and scramble two eggs. Season to taste. Sauté the chopped ham. To ham, add cooked rice, fried onions, green pepper, and scrambled eggs. Mix and heat thoroughly. Soy sauce may be added if desired. Serves 5.

Siamese Fried Beans

1 onion
2 tbsp. cooking oil
2 cups cooked lima beans
2 cups cooked string beans
1 can tomato sauce
½ cup large kernel corn
½ tsp. paprika
dash cayenne pepper
½ tsp. salt

Fry onion in oil until a golden brown.   Add other ingredients.   Serve piping hot.   Serves 6.

Curried Prawns Malayan

1 sliced onion
1 tbsp. butter
2 tbsp. curry paste
2 tbsp. minced ginger
salt to taste
1 chili pepper, chopped
    fine
½ cup consommé
1 cucumber, cubed
1 lb. prawns (cleaned)
juice of 1 lemon
pinch cayenne pepper
1 cup milk

Fry onion until a golden brown. To the consommé, add curry paste, ginger, salt, and chili pepper. Add to onion. Simmer for 15 minutes. Then add cucumber, prawns, lemon juice, and cayenne. Add milk; stew until tender. Serve over hot fluffy rice. Serves 6.

Malayan Dinner

1 stewing hen
1 small onion, chopped
1 cup milk
1 tsp. curry powder
salt and pepper to taste
1 tbsp. flour
½ cup water
cooked rice
chopped onions
chopped tomatoes
chopped celery
chopped cucumber
chopped hard-boiled eggs
chopped peanuts
crushed pineapple
sliced bananas
grated coconut

Stew hen in 1 quart of water until the meat falls off the bones. Add chopped onion for flavoring. Cut the chicken meat into small pieces. To the chicken soup stock, add milk, salt and pepper, and curry powder. Make a paste of flour and water and add to the soup stock. Add more curry powder if needed. Simmer gravy until piping hot. Add cubed chicken. Spoon the chicken and gravy over hot, fluffy, cooked rice. Add on top, layer by layer, the following ingredients: onions, tomatoes, celery, cucumbers, hard-boiled eggs, peanuts, pineapple, bananas, coconut. Serves 8.

Singapore Pudding

½ cup tapioca
2 cups milk
¼ cup sugar
rind of ½ lemon
2 large baked apples
2 eggs
½ cup crushed pineapple
¹/₃ cup cream
½ tsp. nutmeg
½ tsp. cinnamon

Place the tapioca in a double boiler. Add the milk, sugar, and lemon rind. Cook until tapioca becomes tender. Run the baked apples through a sieve; add pulp of apples to tapioca. Separate the eggs and add beaten yolks to tapioca. Add pineapple, cream, and spices. Beat the whites of the egg until stiff and fold into the tapioca. Pour into a buttered baking dish. Bake slowly ½ hour. Serve hot with a dash of whipped cream flavored with sherry. Serves 4.

Ceylon Surprise Cocktail

1 avocado
1 fresh grapefruit
(or canned)

Peel and cube ripe avocado. Peel and divide the grapefruit into segments; remove the seeds. Mix together in a bowl 1 cup of mayonnaise, ½ cup of chili sauce, juice of ½ lemon. Add the fruit to this mixture. Serve in fruit cocktail glasses. Shrimp may be added to this cocktail. Chill and serve. Serves 6.

Colombo Coconut Cup

1 can pineapple, cubed
4 bananas, cubed

1 orange, sliced (remove the seeds)
½ cup grated coconut, toasted

Mix fruit. Serve in fruit cocktail glasses. Sprinkle toasted coconut over top. Serves 6.

Rangoon Stuffed Tomatoes

6 tomatoes, large, peeled
1 cup shrimps, cleaned
½ cup mayonnaise
$1/3$ cup crushed pineapple

Cut tops off tomatoes; scoop out cores. Mix the other
ingredients together and use as stuffing. Serves 6.

Jakarta Delight

6 bananas
1 cup orange juice
1 cup brown sugar
½ cup grated coconut

½ cup dry bread crumbs
(or cake crumbs)
¼ tsp. nutmeg
¼ tsp. cinnamon

Place split bananas in buttered baking dish. Mix orange juice and sugar and pour over the bananas. Mix together crumbs, coconut, and spices. Sprinkle over top. Bake for 20 minutes. Serves 6.

Pineapple and Rum a la Karachi

1 fresh pineapple   **¼ cup sugar**
1 jigger rum

Cut top off pineapple. Run sharp knife around edge inside of pineapple, loosening the fruit from sides. Scoop out and cut into cubes. Place cubed pineapple into a bowl; add sugar and rum. Mix thoroughly. Place the cubed pineapple back inside the shell. Put top back on pineapple and place in refrigerator to chill. To serve, remove top and spoon into fruit cocktail glasses.

About herself, the author has this to say . . .

I guess I should blame all this on Grandfather. While I never met the gentleman, through him I inherited my itchy feet. Honest Asa, as Grandfather was called, had been a master of his own ship that sailed out of Boston to travel the sea lanes of the world.

As a small child I can remember my father showing me maps that once belonged to Grandfather, and listening to the tales that Father spun of the exploits of Honest Asa.

It was then that I became acquainted for the first time with the Sandwich Islands, and later I lived there and grew to love those islands, now called the Hawaiian Islands.

I also heard of Commodore Perry and his Black Fleet which had opened Japan to the outside world, for Grandfather had sailed with Perry. Little did I know at that time that one day I would be trodding on the same ground.

I have always been most grateful for my itchy feet, for without them I would never have left my native California, moved lock, stock, and barrel to Japan, lived in Okinawa, visited China and Thailand, and been able to number among my friends White Russians, Chinese, Japanese, Filipinos, Siamese, Hawaiians, Koreans, and Okinawans.

I am a writer by choice, and a Personnel Officer by necessity. I have been in the Far East with the Army since 1949. Prior to that time I was in radio. I have one daughter, Nancy.

RECIPES FROM THE EAST

HERE is the gourmet's bridge of good will between the East and West. Designed to appeal to the taste of a connoisseur, yet presented with rare clarity, these recipes capture the quintessence of good eating from Karachi to Harbin and from Tokyo to Bali.

These culinary masterpieces of the East, though authentic versions of age-old and beloved delicacies, can all be prepared from materials readily available to the American housewife. Any host or hostess will be proud to add these epicurean treasures to his cooking repertory.

The witty and attractive four-color illustrations accompanying each recipe and the practical spiral binding, which allows the book to remain open at any desired page, make this the ideal gift for any occasion, as well as an invaluable addition to the library of the discriminating housewife or amateur *chef de cuisine*.

The author, IRMA WALKER ROSS, started recipe-collecting as a hobby, the way other people collect stamps. In her avid search for the best recipes from the Orient, she has travelled through many countries and has tested every recipe on her numerous friends, both Occidental and Oriental, who willingly served as her guinea pigs. The present collection contains those recipes which were most popular and for which requests were so overwhelming that Mrs. Ross had no alternative but to go to press with her discoveries.

Charles E. Tuttle Company : Publishers